A HEALING HEART

ASA RAY HENSON

FIRST PRINTING: 2019 ISBN 978-1-79484-135-2

FORWARD ALL INQUIRIES TO THE FOLLOWING:
ASARAYWRITES@GMAIL.COM
ASA RAY HENSON
P.O. BOX 81
ROYSTON, GA 30662

OTHER BOOKS BY ASA RAY HENSON

UNSETTLED & UNSAID

GHOST LETTERS

DEAR RAXLEY

WRITER'S BLOCK

LOVING DAISIES

RED

PROMPT ME TO PROMPT YOU

ROYAL OVERDOSE

SURVIVING 24

FROM THE OUTSIDE LOOKING IN

LIFE IS THE CLOSEST THING TO A LIVING FAIRYTALE AS WE CAN GET. WE HAVE THE ABILITY TO BE ANYTHING WE WANT, LOVE AS MUCH AS WE WISH, AND ACHIEVE ANY GOAL WE SET. I HOPE YOU FIND WAYS TO LIVE OUT YOUR FAIRYTALE EACH DAY, AND I HOPE YOUR HEART ALWAYS HEALS.

WE SAT BENEATH STARS WATCHING EACH OTHER INSTEAD OF THE SKY

AS IF WE COULD MAKE A WISH

RIGHT THERE TOGETHER

AND NEVER HAVE TO LEAVE THE MOMENT

YOU WERE A SHOOTING STAR FULL OF LOVE

WHILE I NEVER UNDERSTOOD HOW GREAT THAT KIND OF LOVE COULD BE

A LOVE DOESN'T HAVE TO LAST FOREVER TO BE DEEP

LIKE A SHOOTING STAR, IT MUST ALWAYS TRAVEL

TRAVEL BACK MY STARLIGHT

SHE WAS AS LIGHT AS WINTER SNOW BEGINNING TO FALL

BLOWING THROUGH THE AIR WITH A JOY SO ADDICTING

YOU COULDN'T HELP BUT FOLLOW

I HAVE LIVED A LIFE OF FEAR

SCARED OF LOVE

TERRIFIED OF ACCEPTING THE ONE THING I WISHED EVERYONE ELSE WOULD ACCEPT ME FOR

THAT IF I KISSED A GIRL, BROUGHT HER HOME, ASKED HER TO MARRY ME

SOMEHOW IT WOULD BE INADEQUATE

THE WORDS OF OUTSIDERS WOULD GET TO ME

THEIR JUDGMENT WOULD RAIN DOWN

AND I WOULD BE UNABLE TO FULFILL THE DUTIES OF LOVING HER WELL ENOUGH

THAT I WOULDN'T BE ABLE TO SUPPORT HER THE WAY I WISHED

PERHAPS SHE WOULD GET HURT FOR LOVING ME

AND I WOULD BE TO BLAME

I AM TIRED OF RUNNING FROM A PLATFORM OF FALSE IDEAS

I SIMPLY WISH TO LOVE A GIRL AND HAVE HER LOVE ME

RISK IT ALL

KISSING IS MY FAVORITE

THE WAY IT CAN BE SO SOFT YET SO ROUGH

YOU COULD KISS ME AND SPILL OUT THE SECRETS OF A LIFETIME

YOUR LIPS WOULD TELL ME YOUR STORY

I LOVE HOW INTRICATE A KISS CAN BE

I LOVE HOW IT CAN MEAN EVERYTHING

LIFE IS A VALUE WE CLING TO EVEN WHEN WE DON'T WANT TO

WE ARE ALWAYS CHASING IT

I HOPE I NEVER STOP

I HAVE FOUND PEACE IN STUDYING

AS IF IT COULD TURN OFF MY MIND TO THE THINGS GOING ON AROUND ME

A MOMENTARY FIX

WHEN I AM LEARNING, I CAN BREATHE

THE THOUGHTS BECOME QUIET VOICES AND I FEEL FEARLESS

PEOPLE THAT DON'T HAVE DEPRESSION DON'T UNDERSTAND

THERE ARE NO RULES

IT'S NOT SOMETHING THAT YOU 'GET AGAIN'

NOT SOMETHING THAT 'COMES BACK'

IT IS ALWAYS WITH YOU

THEY FIND OUT YOU'RE DEPRESSED AND ANY MOMENT YOU TAKE A SECOND TO BREATHE THEY ASSUME YOU'RE NO LONGER OKAY

IT IS TIRING BEING QUESTIONED WHEN I JUST WISH TO CLOSE MY EYES FOR A MOMENT

TO BREATHE

THAT'S NOT ABNORMAL

I WISH THEY UNDERSTOOD

IT'S FUNNY HOW MAKING TIME FOR YOURSELF CAN FEEL LIKE A CHORE

WE PUT SO MUCH PRESSURE ON HOW WE TREAT OTHERS,

BUT WE FORGET HOW TO TREAT OURSELVES

HERE'S TO NORMALIZING BEING KIND TO OURSELVES

WITH SCRAPED KNEES I PUSHED MYSELF OFF THE GROUND,

NOT BOTHERING TO WIPE THEM OFF

IT WAS ABOUT TIME I STOPPED CLEANING MY WOUNDS AND SIMPLY KEPT MOVING

SOMETIMES THAT'S ALL IT SEEMS YOU CAN DO

OTHERWISE YOU GET YOUR HAIR CAUGHT IN A

WINDMILL OF SELF DESTRUCTIVE CYCLES AND

WHO HAS TIME FOR THAT NOWADAYS

NOT WHEN THERE'S A NEW DOOR TO WALK THROUGH

A NEW OPPORTUNITY AROUND THE CORNER

AS I WORK ON CAPTIONING VIDEOS CLIENTS HAVE SENT ME, I FEEL AS IF I AM CAPTIONING MY LIFE. PASTING WORDS ON A SCREEN OF VIDEOS TO PLAY BACK THE THINGS I'VE EXPERIENCED. SOME OF IT IS PURE LAUGHTER, OTHER PIECES ARE A HEADACHE, BUT I AM CONTENT IN FINDING BITS OF MYSELF AMONGST THE CAPTIONS. LIKE ECHOES OF WHO I HAVE BEEN, FOR THE WORLD TO SEE.

WE LIKE TO THINK WE'RE SOMETHING SPECIAL, AND IN SOME WAYS WE ARE. WE'RE DIFFERENT WHILE SOMEHOW BEING THE SAME. OUR SPECIAL QUIRKS MAKE US RELATABLE, ADMIRABLE EVEN. YET WE DEAL WITH PAIN AND SUFFERING THE SAME. WE REACT TO HAPPY MOMENTS THE SAME. WE MAY HAVE TRAITS AND LITTLE DOTS OF OUR PERSONALITY THAT REMAINS SOLELY OURS, BUT WHEN WE FEEL WE EMBRACE OUR EMOTIONS THE SAME. WE ARE ONE WHILE BEING MANY.

SHE WANTED LOVE. LOVE FOR HERSELF, HER HOME, FOR EVERYTHING. SHE WANTED LOVE FROM HER FRIENDS AND FAMILY, THE WORLD, AND SHE WANTED IT FROM HERSELF. EVERYTHING SHE DID WAS OUT OF LOVE. WHETHER IT APPEARED THAT WAY OR NOT. ALL SHE WANTED WAS TO LOVE AND BE LOVED. HOW SIMPLE IT SHOULD'VE BEEN.

YOU CAN FIND MY HEART WRITTEN BETWEEN PAGES OF WORDS,

FLOATING BETWEEN THE LETTERS THAT HANG AND SMILING BEHIND THE MEANINGS OF STORIES

WHENEVER YOU NEED ME NEAR, SIMPLY PICK UP A BOOK AND OPEN IT

YOU'LL FIND ME, CRYSTAL CLEAR.

PLEASE ASK FOR HELP WHEN YOU FEEL LIKE GIVING UP. RATHER THAN TURNING THE SHOWER COLD AND LETTING YOUR TEARS WASH AWAY, REACH OUT FOR HELP. IT DOES NOT MAKE YOU LESS OF A PERSON TO NEED SOMEBODY BESIDE YOU SOMETIMES. YOU ARE BEYOND WORDS VALUE, AND YOU NEVER DESERVE TO FACE THE HARSHNESS OF BEING ISOLATED OR ALONE.

SHE BEGGED FOR ME TO COME BACK.

AT SOME POINT IN MY LIFE I WOULD'VE.

BUT I DIDN'T WHEN SHE ASKED.

I TURNED MY HEAD THE OPPOSITE DIRECTION AND WALKED FURTHER AWAY.

YOU SEE, I HAD PROMISED HER THE WORLD.

I HAD GIVEN HER MY LOYALTY.

BUT SHE WAS ON SUCH A PATH OF UNCERTAINTY, SHE COULDN'T DO THE SAME.

HER LOVE FOR ME WAS SELFISH.

SHE ONLY BEGGED FOR MY RETURN WHEN SHE WAS

 IN NEED OF SOMETHING SHE COULDN'T GET FROM SOMEBODY ELSE.

I DON'T REGRET WALKING AWAY OR BREAKING MY PROMISES.

I DON'T REGRET LOVING MYSELF MORE THAN I LOVED HER.

LOOKING BACK AT THE PEOPLE THAT'VE LEFT MY LIFE, I FEEL A VOLCANO OF EMOTIONS. IT'S AS IF I HAVE SUCH FOND MOMENTS WITH THEM, NO MATTER HOW THE RELATIONSHIP ENDED. I LOOK AT THE TIMES WE HAD AND I AM GRATEFUL. I SMILE OVER THE MOMENTS WE SHARED. THE STUPID FIGHTS. ALL OF IT. I AM GLAD THEY ARE A PIECE OF WHO I AM AND WHO I WILL BECOME.

TEENS ARE PLACING BOTTLES TO THEIR LIPS AND I AM WATCHING SILENT AS MY THOUGHTS WASH INTO A STATE OF SORROW FOR THEM

FOR THE PARENTS THAT HAVE GIVEN THEM A BREW THEY DON'T KNOW THE DANGERS OF

FOR THE HABITS THEY ARE CREATING AT SUCH A YOUNG AGE

THEY ARE SMALL, FRAGILE, EASILY ENTERTAINED

AS THEY TAKE EACH SIP, SWALLOW DOWN THE BURN

I PITY THEM

THEIR LIGHTHEARTED LAUGHTER IS THE MATCH TO A FIRE THEY'LL BURN THE REST OF THEIR LIVES

I AM SORRY FOR THAT

FLOWER PETAL WORDS FEEL SOFT AGAINST MY SKIN

ACTING AS REMINDERS THAT I AM OKAY

BECOMING FRIENDS DANCING ALONG THE INSIDE OF MY MIND

I AM A WHORE FOR THE KIND MOMENTS

THE GENTLE ENCOURAGEMENT

PLEASE, GIVE ME MORE

IT MOTIVATES ME

LATE AT NIGHT I CAN STILL FEEL YOUR LEGS WRAPPED AROUND ME

PULLING ME AS CLOSE AS HUMANLY POSSIBLE

I CAN HEAR YOUR WHISPERS AND FEEL THE TUG OF YOUR TEETH ON MY EAR AS YOU FILL ME WITH EMPTY PROMISES

IN SOME WAYS I BELIEVE I LOVED YOU SO MUCH BECAUSE YOU REMINDED ME OF THE DARKNESS INSIDE OF ME

I COULD FOCUS ON YOUR STRUGGLES AND AVOID FACING MY OWN

IN MOST WAYS I CAN ONLY ENTERTAIN THE THOUGHT OF WHY I LOVED YOU SO HARD BECAUSE WHEN I LOOK AT YOU NOW,

I DON'T FEEL LOVE

I NO LONGER FEEL COMPASSION

I DON'T HATE YOU AND I HAVE NO MALICE TOWARDS YOU,

BUT I LOOK AT YOU AND I FEEL NOTHING

I AM NUMB

LONG NIGHTS LEAD TO THOUGHTS OF MY FUTURE

OF WRAPPING MYSELF BETWEEN YOUR ARMS AND FINDING COMFORT

SIPPING COFFEE IN THE MORNINGS WITH TINY MARSHMALLOWS, WHO DOESN'T LOVE THAT CHILDLIKE JOY?

I FALL ASLEEP CRAVING THE SOFTNESS OF YOUR HANDS DRAWING SHAPES ON MY SKIN IN THE MOST INNOCENT WAYS

I FIND DELIGHT IN THE SIMPLE THOUGHTS

OF FINDING YOU IN A HAPPILY EVER AFTER FILLED WITH GROWTH AND SHARING

I LOOK FORWARD TO OPENING THE CAGE OF MY HEART AND LETTING YOU FEED IT.

THIS YEAR HAS BEEN FILLED WITH GROWTH

LIFE LESSON AFTER LIFE LESSONS

I HAVE HAD TO LEARN PATIENCE WITH MYSELF

HOW TO REBUILD MY ENTIRETY AFTER MY EMOTIONS HAVE SWALLOWED ME WHOLE AND SPIT ME BACK OUT

THERE HAVE BEEN DAYS WHEN I CURLED UP ONLY TO CRY UNTIL I SLEPT THE NIGHT AWAY

SOMEHOW I HAVE MADE IT THOUGH

I HAVE LIVED THROUGH THE STORMS

DODGED THE HURRICANES ENOUGH TO RESTRUCTURE MY LITTLE WORLD

IT HAS BEEN EXHAUSTING YET FULFILLING

I MAY NOT BE RUNNING WILD AND RAMPANT,

BUT I AM FINDING JOY WITHIN THE SMALL BITS OF WHO I AM

I AM TAKING THE CHAPTERS OF LIFE ONE STEP AT A TIME, WATCHING AS THEY WRITE THEMSELVES

I am evolving

YOU WILL FIND YOURSELF FACING DAYS WHERE THE SUN DOESN'T SHINE AND YOU CAN'T FIND A SINGLE THING TO SHOW YOU BRIGHTNESS,

BE YOUR OWN SUNSHINE DURING THOSE DAYS,

CREATE YOUR OWN LIGHT AND LET THE PEOPLE AROUND YOU LATHER IN YOUR WARMTH

YOU ARE PURE RADIANCE WHEN YOU WISH TO BE.

REMEMBER TO ALWAYS LOVE YOURSELF FIRST

YOU DESERVE THE GOODNESS OF YOUR OWN HEART

DARLING,

YOU MUST REMEMBER YOU ARE NEVER AS SMALL AS YOU FEEL. PEOPLE WILL MAKE YOU FEEL TINY IN THEIR PRESENCE. THEY WILL INTIMIDATE YOU AND CREATE THIS IMAGINARY WORLD WHERE YOU ARE NOT ENOUGH. BUT YOU MUST RECALL YOU ARE STRONGER THAN A MOUNTAIN, AS BEAUTIFUL AS NATURE. YOUR NAME TASTES LIKE CHOCOLATE AND YOUR POWER WILL ALWAYS MOVE ACROSS OCEANS LIKE THE WIND. YOU ARE EVERYTHING. DON'T LET THEM DEFLATE YOU BEING A BLESSING.

THE OLDER I GET THE MORE COMFORT I FIND IN NIGHTS SPENT IN

THERE IS A SENSE OF SANITY IN THE SAFETY OF MY HOME

A FORM OF CLARITY

WITH AGE I FIND SATISFACTION WITH INTIMATE MOMENTS SPENT WITH

FRIENDS RATHER THAN STRANGERS IN A CROWD

THERE IS HAPPINESS IN THE LAUGHTER I SHARE WITH THE PEOPLE

I CARE FOR, NOT THE PEOPLE I NEVER KNEW.

LEARN TO EDIT YOURSELF

LIKE A VIDEO IN PREPARATION

A MOVIE WITH SCENES SHOT OVER AND OVER

A BOOK THAT HAS BEEN WRITTEN TO TELL A STORY INTENTIONALLY

YOU CAN MAKE THIS LIFE WHATEVER YOU WISH IT TO BE

LITTLE GIRL DON'T YOU REMEMBER THE PAIN YOU WENT THROUGH? DO YOU REMEMBER THE NIGHTS WITHOUT A HOME? WHAT ABOUT THE SCREAMS THAT FELT SO HARSH YOU COULD'VE USED THEM LIKE GLASS ON YOUR SKIN? DO YOU LOOK BACK AT THOSE MOMENTS WITH REGRET? DO YOU STILL FEAR THE SOUND OF YOUR OWN VOICE? I AM SORRY YOU HAD TO GROW UP IN A HOME OF UNCERTAINTY. I AM SORRY YOU WERE SILENCED WHEN ALL YOU WANTED TO DO WAS YELL. I HOPE YOU'RE DOING WELL OUT IN THE WORLD. I HOPE YOU'RE FINDING YOURSELF AND YOUR VOICE. STAY SAFE, LITTLE ONE.

I FIND IT FUNNY HOW WE WAIT FOR A NEW YEAR TO APPROACH BEFORE

SETTING GOALS OR PLANNING A 'FRESH START'.

WE HAVE THE ABILITY TO RECREATE OURSELVES AT ANY GIVEN MOMENT

YET WE ONLY GIVE OURSELVES ON DAY PER YEAR TO DO SO

STOP BEING SO HARD ON YOURSELF

HIT THE RESTART BUTTON WHENEVER YOU WANT

MAKE A WAY TO BECOME WHOEVER YOU WISH TO BE ANY MOMENT

YOU ARE CAPABLE OF CREATION WHENEVER YOU WISH

STOP HOLDING BACK

YOU ARE YOUR OWN LIMIT

RECENTLY I LEARNED THAT EUNOIA STOOD FOR A WELL MIND OR BEAUTIFUL THINKING

I HEARD THE WORD A KNEW IT WAS SOMETHING SPECIAL

AS THE DAYS PASS, I CRAVE FOR MOMENTS OF EUNOIA

FOR HEALTH

FOR BEAUTIFUL THOUGHTS

I HOPE YOU FEEL EUNOIA EVERY SINGLE DAY

STOP MAKING A HOME A PLACE

YES, A HOUSE IS NICE TO HAVE

A PLACE TO GO TO IN ORDER TO UNWIND IS A MUST

BUT YOU WILL ALWAYS BE YOUR HOME

MAKE SURE YOU RELY ON YOURSELF TOO

LIFE ISN'T ABOUT THE DESTINATION OR THE JOURNEY,

IT'S ABOUT HOW YOU MAKE THE TWO WORK

PICK OUT THE DESTINATION YOU WANT TO REACH EACH DAY, WEEK, MONTH

AND EMBRACE THE JOURNEY THAT GETS YOU THERE

YOU ARE THE REASON THE JOURNEY AND DESTINATION EXIST

THERE IS A CALMNESS EARLY IN THE MORNING

BEFORE THE REST OF THE WORLD HAS BECOME ROWDY WITH THE DAY

YOU CAN FIND A HAPPINESS MINGLING IN THE AIR EARLY ON

WAITING FOR YOU TO SAY HI WITH YOUR FIRST CUP OF THE DAY

GIGGLING AT YOUR SLEEPY THOUGHTS

YOUR INNOCENT MANNERISMS

ANY CHANCE YOU GET TO HANG FOR A MOMENT WITH THOSE EARLY MORNINGS

TAKE IT

PEOPLE HAVE A TENDENCY TO TELL YOU WHAT YOU CAN DO

WHO YOU CAN BE

WHAT YOU WILL DO WITH YOUR LIFE

FUCK THOSE PEOPLE

THEY ARE SO BUSY DETERMINING THE WAYS YOU SHOULD LIVE FOR THEM

THAT THEY'RE FORGETTING TO LIVE FOR THEMSELVES

TAKE THERE WORDS AND BURN THEM LIKE A LOG AT A BONFIRE

BE WHO YOU WISH TO BE

DO WHAT YOU WANT TO DO

YOUR LIFE IS YOURS AND ONLY YOURS

DON'T WASTE IT PLEASING THE WORLD WITHOUT PLEASING YOURSELF

TIME TRULY DOES HEAL

WITH THE RIGHT CLOCKWORK YOU WILL RECOVER FROM THE WORST OF INJURIES

YOU MAY FALL AND SCRAPE YOUR KNEES, BUT IN TIME YOU'LL ONLY BE LEFT WITH A SCAR

YOUR HEART WILL BREAK OVER LOVE, LAUGHTER, AND A MILLION OTHER TINY MINUTES

YET THE BEST CLOCKWORK WILL HAVE YOUR WOUNDED HEART BEATING IN NO TIME

TIME IS ALWAYS THERE

ALWAYS BANDAGING AND HEALING

EVEN IF YOU TRY TO PUSH IT AWAY

SOCIETY HAS DECLARED WHO I SHOULD LOVE

IT HAS DEEMED THAT I SHOULD NOT KISS THE PRETTY GIRL

REGARDLESS OF THE DOTS THIS UNIVERSE HAS CONNECTED,

SOCIETY HAS DECIDED WHO IS FIT AND WHO'S UNFIT TO BE TOGETHER

I AM TIRED OF HOLDING BACK MY WORDS

OF SWALLOWING THE I LOVE YOU'S

IT MAKES ME SICK TO TELL SOMEBODY WE ARE JUST FRIENDS

I WANT TO HOLD YOUR HAND IN THE STREETS

I WANT TO KISS YOU AS WE LAUGH OVER THE SILLY PARTS OF LIFE

WHEN YOU'VE TAKEN A SIP OF YOUR MILKSHAKE AND HAVE A

SPECKLE OF WHITE CREAM ON YOUR NOSE

I WANT TO LOOK AT YOU IN AWE AND DECLARE HOW FUCKING BEAUTIFUL YOU ARE

SOCIETY CAN TAKE THE NEED FOR CONTROL AND PUSH IT BACK ON THEMSELVES

I WILL SPEND A LIFETIME FALLING IN LOVE WITH YOU AND SHOWING IT

I WANT TO LEARN EVERY LANGUAGE IN THE WORLD SOLELY

TO WHISPER MY LOVE TO YOU IN EACH ONE.

OBSESS WITH YOURSELF THE WAY YOU OBSESS WITH A TV SHOW

YOU ARE AS BEAUTIFUL AS ANY IDOL YOU SEE

NO MATTER WHAT YOU WEAR

REGARDLESS OF THE PEOPLE YOU HANG OUT WITH

MAKE UP OR NOT

TREAT YOURSELF WITH THAT SAME EXCITEMENT AND

FIND THE QUALITIES THAT MAKE YOU SO EASILY LOVABLE

TRAVELING HAS A WAY OF OPENING THE SOUL TO NEW THINGS

MAKE TIME TO DISCOVER THE WORLD

SAVE MONEY TO VISIT CITY AFTER CITY

OPEN YOUR EYES AND SEE SOMETHING OUTSIDE OF YOUR BUBBLE

THERE IS MORE OUT THERE THAN THE TOWN YOU GREW UP IN

GET ON THE FLIGHT

THE BOAT

SEE SOMETHING MAGICAL DUDE

DEAR FUTURE,

I AM EXCITED TO HAVE YOU FALL ASLEEP ON ME. WITH ME. I AM TREMBLING WITH GLEE FOR THE LESSONS WE WILL LEARN FROM EACH OTHER. THE MEALS WE WILL SHARE. OBNOXIOUS SINGING. ADVENTURES AROUND THE WORLD. I CAN'T WAIT TO SEE THE THINGS THIS LIFE HAS TO OFFER US. I'M EXCITED TO INTRODUCE YOU TO MY MOM. MY FAMILY. I'M EXCITED FOR THEM TO LOVE YOU AS MUCH AS I DO. AS MUCH AS I ANTICIPATE THE HAPPIEST MOMENTS WITH YOU, I AM HAPPY WAITING AROUND. I'M CONTENT GROWING ON MY OWN AS LONG AS I NEED TO. WHEN I FIND YOU, I'LL BE READY, BUT I AM NO LESS WITHOUT YOU.
THANK YOU FOR BEING THE FUTURE.

LOSE YOURSELF IN MUSIC

IN BOOKS OF POETRY AND FANTASY

FIND YOURSELF IN THOSE AS WELL

YOU WILL FIND A SECRET BUTTON OF RENEWAL EACH TIME

SHED THE THINGS YOU NO LONGER NEED TO ACCOMPANY YOU IN LIFE AND

WELCOME THE NEW PIECES

YOU ARE A GALAXY IN A WORLD OF GALAXIES

ALWAYS A MYSTERY TO THE OUTSIDE

REMEMBER THAT WHEN YOU FEEL YOUR LIGHT IS DIMMING

THERE ARE MILLIONS OF OTHER STARS WITHIN YOU SHINING